The Gift
of Forgiveness

Denise Renner

The Gift
of Forgiveness

Denise Renner

Unless otherwise indicated, all Scripture quotations are taken from the *King James Version* of the Bible.

The Gift of Forgiveness
ISBN 978-0-9725454-4-0
Copyright © 2004 by Denise Renner
P. O. Box 702040
Tulsa, OK 74170-2040

Published by Harrison House
Shippensburg, PA 17257-2914
www.harrisonhouse.com

14 15 16 17 18 / 24 23 22 21
14th printing 2021

Editorial Consultant: Cynthia D. Hansen
Text Design: Lisa Simpson

Table of Contents

1

The Power
in Forgiveness

God has been strongly dealing with me about my love walk for the past several years. He has especially been dealing with me about allowing forgiveness to flow out of me like a free-flowing river. I know from personal experience that this is infinitely better than allowing offense to remain in me until it becomes a stagnant, foul-smelling, poisonous, filthy pond of resentment, bitterness, and critical attitudes.

Forgiveness is an extremely important issue to God. After all, He sent Jesus to this earth to open a way for us to be forgiven of our sins. And when it comes to our relationships with others, it is the absolute number-one priority on God's list that we become quick to forgive. We are not to waste even five minutes of our time being offended; instead, our hearts are to become a place from which the fresh water of God's love and power continually flows rather than bitterness, resentment, and offense.

> Forgiveness is an extremely important issue to God.

John 20:22 and 23 give us a clue about how important forgiveness is from God's perspective.

And when he [Jesus] had said this, he breathed on them [the disciples], and saith unto them, Receive ye the Holy Ghost:

Whose soever sins ye remit, they are remitted unto them; and whose soever sins ye retain, they are retained.

The moment Jesus said to His disciples, "...Receive ye the Holy Ghost," that was the moment the disciples were born again. And the very next thing Jesus talked about was the subject of forgiveness! Think about it — the very next words that came from Jesus after His disciples received the Spirit were not about evangelism or tithing, but about *forgiveness*.

First, Jesus said, "Whose soever sins ye remit, they are remitted unto them...." This word "remit" means *to send away*. So whenever we choose to forgive someone who has sinned against us, we send that sin away from the offender. But if we refuse to remit that person's sin, it is retained unto him.

This is so amazing! The disciples had just received the Holy Spirit. Jesus had only a few days left on this earth. And the very first thing He said after they received the Holy Spirit was that they had the power to forgive people's sins!

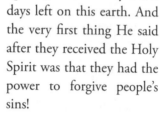

If we refuse to remit that person's sin, it is retained unto him.

If we remit people's sins, they are remitted. But if we retain those offenses — if we refuse to forgive — they are retained. That doesn't mean we are in any way someone's savior. But when it comes to the offenses that a person commits against *us*, we can choose to release those offenses and let that person go free.

This must be a very important truth for us to understand; otherwise, why would it be the first thing Jesus said to His disciples after they were born again? He wanted to show them the power that had come to reside within them in the Person of the Holy Spirit.

The Prison of Unforgiveness

The sins we forgive will be forgiven. But if we do not forgive our brother's sins, they will *not* be forgiven. We can liken this concept to a container with a tight lid. If we close the container and seal the lid, the contents aren't coming out again until we take off the lid.

The same thing happens in the spiritual realm when someone sins against a person and that person chooses to retain that sin through unforgiveness. This means that the responsibility to release the offender from his sin lies with the one who has been sinned against — not with the counseling department, the pastor, or even the offender himself.

For example, suppose a man grew up with an ungodly father who wounded him either physically or emotionally. If that man refuses to forgive his father, carrying those wounds into his adult years, his father's sins against his son will also be retained and will keep the father in a spiritual prison until the son chooses to forgive.

Of course, the father could escape that prison himself through his own decision to repent before God and his son. However, the son's unforgiveness becomes the very thing that hinders the Holy Spirit from working in the father's heart to bring him to repentance!

Or let's take the example of a woman who's praying for her husband to be saved. For years, her husband hasn't treated her right, and she struggles with unforgiveness. Meanwhile, she prays and prays that he will get saved and change. She gets frustrated as time goes by and her prayers don't seem to get answered — not realizing that she is hindering the process herself by holding on to the sins her husband has committed against her.

If that wife doesn't send away her husband's sins, she retains them. As long as she holds on to those sins and refuses to forgive him, those sins remain on him and he is held to his old patterns of action. She can pray 14 more years, but until she releases him through forgiveness, she locks him in a prison that holds him captive to his sin. On the other hand, the moment the wife chooses to forgive, she opens the door for the Holy Ghost to begin to work out God's will in her husband's life.

I remember a Ukrainian woman minister whose unsaved husband had been committing adultery for five years. After she heard this message about forgiveness and what her part was, she saw her own wrong in holding those offenses against her husband. So we prayed together, and she asked God to forgive her for her bitterness. Then she completely forgave and released her husband from the sins he had committed against her.

Four months later, this woman came to me and said, "I have a testimony. I forgave my husband from my heart, and he is now saved and in the ministry with me!"

I'll share another example that happened in our church in Moscow. A young 15-year-old girl heard this message and saw that she needed to release her father from the sins he had committed against her. He was an alcoholic and had been abusive to her in the home when she was very young. As she grew toward adolescence, her heart had hardened against her father so that she refused to see or even talk to him. She hadn't seen him for seven years.

After hearing the Word of God about forgiveness, this young girl prayed and asked God to forgive her for holding offenses against her father. Then God spoke to the girl's heart, instructing her to call her father and ask him to meet her at McDonald's.

They met; she forgave him; and they cried together as God began the healing process in their hearts. And now, after seven years of absolutely no fellowship or contact, this father and daughter meet at least once or twice a week to rebuild their relationship on a new foundation of love and forgiveness.

This is the power that God has given us. When we retain the sins others have committed against us, those sins are retained. We can pray and pray and pray, but if we still hold on to the offenses in our hearts, our unforgiveness releases something in the spirit realm that holds the offenders to their sin.

This young girl could have held her father to his sins for the rest of her life. But if she had done that, she would have lost the sweet fellowship with him that she now enjoys because of the choice she made to forgive.

> **When we retain the sins others have committed against us, those sins are retained.**

There is one more important point to understand about the power that resides in our unforgiveness. It doesn't just bind our offenders to their sins. We also put *ourselves* in a prison whenever we refuse to forgive. As long as our offender remains a captive to his sin, we keep ourselves in our own prison as well.

But, thank God, that isn't the only possible end to the story! Our decision to forgive also releases something in the spirit realm — the delivering power of God! That's why forgiveness is one of the most powerful gifts we can ever give to other people.

Stephen's Example of Forgiveness

Let's look at Jesus' words in John 20:23 again: "Whose soever sins ye remit, they are remitted unto them; and whose soever sins ye retain, they are retained." We can find a great example of this principle in Acts 7:54-60.

In this account, Stephen was very close to death. He had been a bold witness for Jesus, and now the Jewish religious leaders were all gathered around him, ready to stone him to death. And they weren't throwing little pebbles, either — they were throwing big rocks at him to completely crush his skull

> We put *ourselves* in a prison whenever we refuse to forgive.

and kill him. Stephen was just seconds away from seeing Jesus face-to-face. Let's read what happened.

> When they heard these things, they were cut to the heart, and they gnashed on him [Stephen] with their teeth.

> But he, being full of the Holy Ghost, looked up stedfastly into heaven, and saw the glory of God, and Jesus standing on the right hand of God,

> And said, Behold, I see the heavens opened, and the Son of man standing on the right hand of God.

> Then they cried out with a loud voice, and stopped their ears, and ran upon him with one accord,

> And cast him out of the city, and stoned him: and the witnesses laid down their clothes at a young man's feet, whose name was Saul.

And they stoned Stephen, calling upon God, and saying, Lord Jesus, receive my spirit.

And he kneeled down, and cried with a loud voice, Lord, lay not this sin to their charge. And when he had said this, he fell asleep.

In verse 59, Stephen cried out, "…Lord Jesus, receive my spirit." He was just seconds from eternity. But look at the next thing that happened: "And he kneeled down, and cried with a loud voice, Lord, lay not this sin to their charge. And when he had said this, he fell asleep" (v. 60).

Who was in that audience? Acts 8:1 tells us: "And Saul was consenting unto his death…." There stood the future apostle Paul, approving of Stephen's death. And in the last few moments of his life, Stephen removed that sin from him.

I believe with all my heart that Saul was forgiven because Stephen cried out to God and asked Him not to hold the sin to Saul's charge. Think about this power that believers have been given to remit another's sin. Just seconds before Stephen left this life to enter God's presence, he cried out, "Lord, lay it not to their charge!" And in that one act, Stephen released the future apostle Paul to fulfill his own destiny in God!

Jesus activated the same spiritual principle as He hung dying on the Cross. He cried out, "...Father, forgive them; for they know not what they do..." (Luke 23:34). Jesus' forgiveness made a way for His offenders to be saved!

Most Christians don't realize the kind of power they have in the spirit realm — a power that can operate both positively and negatively. For instance, several people could be having a wonderful time talking to one another, but if another person enters the scene who is angry and upset, the entire atmosphere and conversation often changes to fit the angry person's mood.

Our attitudes affect people — and an attitude of unforgiveness is especially powerful. When we don't forgive, we hold people in the place they are in. They are hindered from changing and going further in God because we have kept them tied to their sin.

Let's go back to Stephen and consider the eternal significance of the moment described in verse 60. He only had mere seconds before he would leave this life; yet he used those seconds to forgive his offenders.

> When we don't forgive, we hold people in the place they are in.

These few seconds carried much importance for the future apostle Paul and for Stephen. Stephen didn't want to die with unforgiveness in his heart. Huge stones were being hurled at him. He was bleeding, in great pain, and sensing that his life would slip from him in mere moments. Yet in the midst of all this, he found the strength to say, "God, forgive them!"

Stephen didn't know the future apostle Paul was standing in that crowd, consenting to and even enjoying the spectacle of his death. But because Stephen was willing to forgive, the man who would become the apostle Paul never had to be forgiven of that sin, for Stephen sent it away from him through forgiveness.

I believe that Stephen had a great deal to do with the future ministry of the great apostle Paul, who stood by watching the stoning in complete approval. It was vitally important that Stephen chose to forgive Paul so God's purposes could be fulfilled in Paul's life.

Our Responsibility To Release Others Through Forgiveness

We need to forgive just as quickly as Stephen did. When our offenders are throwing stones at us, we must immediately free them and not hold it to their charge.

If God is calling you to release someone in your life, don't try to change that person. Choose to forgive him so you can see him walking in freedom one day. It is so vitally important that you forgive quickly and refuse to hold on to offense.

Just think — what if Stephen had held on to the sin of his offenders? In a few seconds, it would have been too late for Stephen to forgive.

Could it be that if Stephen hadn't forgiven, Saul would not have been released to fulfill his calling as the apostle Paul, and the entire history of the Early Church would have been adversely affected?

God has given you a tremendous responsibility in this power to remit or to retain sin. If you are having a struggle with unforgiveness, consider this:

- *What call is on the person's life whom you are refusing to forgive? You may not know, but neither did Stephen know about Saul's calling; he just forgave.*

- *If that person was released from the prison of your unforgiveness to answer his call, how many lives would he or she touch for God's Kingdom?*

As it gets darker and darker out in the world, God is calling us to shine brighter and brighter with the glory of His light and love by learning to be better forgivers and releasers. But as long as we allow unforgiveness to stay in us, we keep the door open for darkness and deception to slip in. Certainly it is for the benefit of the offender and the call of God on his life that we release him from his sin. But it is also for *our* benefit that we forgive when we are offended.

> If God is calling you to release someone in your life, don't try to change that person.

Let's cry out to God to make us more like Stephen. Let's develop an urgency in our spirits to *immediately* release people at the moment of offense. Let it never be said that we are responsible for holding *one person* captive in the prison of past offenses or sins!

2

Divine Lessons
on Forgiveness

*M*atthew 18 relates a very significant teaching session on forgiveness that Peter initiated when he asked Jesus, "How many times do I have to forgive my brother?" Pay close attention to how Jesus responded to that question, for if you're anything like me, you've asked a similar question at one time or another in your life!

Jesus' response to Peter's question was definitely *not* an answer that caters to our flesh; nevertheless, His words contain a vital key to our ultimate freedom and success in life:

> Then came Peter to him, and said, Lord, how oft shall my brother sin against me, and I forgive him? till seven times?
>
> Jesus saith unto him, I say not unto thee, Until seven times: but, Until seventy times seven.
>
> Matthew 18:21,22

Jesus wasn't giving Peter a specific number of times he needed to forgive his brother. Jesus was actually saying, "*Never* stop forgiving until I come again!"

'How Many Times Do I Have To Forgive?'

Growing up in Miami, Oklahoma, I loved God as much as I could love Him. I was raised in a denominational church that didn't believe in the baptism in the Holy Spirit, so I just kept rededicating my life and told God I was willing to be a missionary. That was as spiritual as I thought I could get, and I was trying *hard*!

As a teenager in high school, I continued to live the best I knew how for Jesus. I didn't drink; I didn't smoke; and I kept my virginity until marriage. But because I made these kinds of decisions for my life, I didn't have many friends.

There was another girl at the school who also didn't have any friends, so she and I formed a friendship of sorts and hung out together. She and I went through high school and junior college together, and since we were both involved in music as singers, we attended many of the same classes.

This girl didn't drink or smoke either; however, she also didn't treat me well at all! I'll give

you just one small example. She was more orga-
nized than I was, so sometimes when I came to
choir, she'd have her music and I wouldn't. But
as we stood next to each other singing, she'd
deliberately move her music so it was hidden
from my view. Because she claimed to be my
friend, it was a great put-down when she did
things like this to me. I really felt as if these
things were designed to make me feel like I
wasn't as good as she was.

Today as I look back, I realize that I had a
lot of character defects in my own personality
at that time and that this girl was a beautiful,
talented person who was probably as lonely as
I was. I'm sure now that our friendship would
have been totally different if I had felt better
about myself; however, I was walking in all the
revelation I had at the time, and so was she. But
let's get back to my story.

No matter how ugly the girl acted toward
me, I'd just take it and forgive her. After all, it

wasn't as if I had a lot of other friends to replace her with!

This went on for five years — all the way through high school and junior college. Then God told me to go to the University of Oklahoma. Going to OU would have been fine with me, except that I knew *she* was going there too. Since we were both majoring in music, I realized that we'd be in all the same classes, and the bad treatment would start all over again.

I had already suffered under this person's persecution for years, and I didn't want to do it any longer. I didn't want to forgive her anymore. I reasoned that if she went to one university and I went somewhere else, I wouldn't have to forgive her because she'd be out of my life.

> I didn't want to forgive her anymore.

So I went to Oklahoma Baptist University instead — where I spent the most miserable year of my life because I had disobeyed God's plan. At some point in that school year, I repented of my disobedience and determined to get back in God's will. The next fall, I was admitted to the University of Oklahoma.

Just as I expected, my "friend" was in all my classes, and she still treated me the same way. I thought to myself, *I can't believe it. This isn't high school anymore. I'm in my twenties, and she still treats me the same rotten way!*

So I went to someone whom I considered to be more spiritual than I and told him about my predicament. I asked him, "Do I have to just keep on forgiving her?" I bet you can guess what his response was.

"Yes, you must forgive."

Now, I already knew that I had to forgive this girl, but I was just like Peter. I was asking, "But *how many times* do I have to forgive her?"

When Jesus told Peter that he needed to forgive someone "seventy times seven," Peter probably thought, *Seventy times seven is A LOT to forgive!* I knew exactly how Peter must have felt, because Jesus was actually saying, "Just keep on forgiving and forgiving and forgiving and forgiving *forever*."

To make a long story short, I finally got my heart right and forgave this precious young woman unconditionally. Gradually she started treating me better. Later she even sent Rick and me a wedding present when we got married!

I learned that my precious friend wasn't my problem — it was *my own attitude of unforgiveness*. It certainly is a human trait to ask, "How long do I have to forgive?" But Jesus will never change His answer: *"Until I come again."*

Redeemed From
Satan's Slave Market

In Matthew 18:23-35, Jesus continued teaching His disciples on the subject of forgiveness with a parable we can all relate to. The parable began with a profound act of mercy:

> Therefore is the kingdom of heaven likened unto a certain king, which would take account of his servants.
>
> And when he had begun to reckon, one was brought unto him, which owed him ten thousand talents.
>
> But forasmuch as he had not to pay, his lord commanded him to be sold, and his wife, and children, and all that he had, and payment to be made.
>
> The servant therefore fell down, and worshipped him, saying, Lord, have patience with me, and I will pay thee all.

> Then the lord of that servant was moved with compassion, and loosed him, and forgave him the debt.
>
> Matthew 18:23-27

Verse 24 says that this servant owed the king 10,000 talents. Today that is the equivalent of about 290 million dollars — an enormous debt that the man could never hope to pay back!

Let's apply this servant's plight to our own lives. What is the one thing we can't buy, no matter how rich we are? It is impossible for us to buy *a gift*, because a gift is free. Well, that is exactly what our salvation is — a free gift. Like the servant, we had a debt of sin we could not pay. There was absolutely *nothing* we could do to pay it. And just as this servant received mercy from the king, the Lord paid *our* debt when we asked Him for mercy: "Then the lord of that servant was moved with compassion, and loosed him, and forgave him the debt" (v. 27).

Matthew 18:25 tells us that the servant and his entire family escaped slavery because of his master's forgiveness: "But forasmuch as he had not to pay, his lord commanded him to be sold, and his wife, and children, and all that he had, and payment to be made." That's what happened with us as well. God was moved with compassion to save us from spiritual slavery by sending His Son Jesus to pay the debt of sin we couldn't pay. In fact, the word "redeemed" actually means *to buy from slavery.*

> Just as this servant received mercy from the king, the Lord paid our debt when we asked Him for mercy.

I want to describe to you what a slave market in biblical times was like. First, of course, there were the slaves. Then there were those who came to buy the slaves. Finally, there was the slaveowner.

The slave would have to just stand there with all the other slaves while the buyers examined him in any way they saw fit. For instance, a buyer might kick, slap, or beat him in an effort to get the slave to react. If the slave withstood the beating without reacting, he would be considered a good slave who could take a lot of abuse, and his price would go up. The buyer might also look inside the slave's mouth to see if he had gold teeth. After all, the buyer was looking to get the most for his money!

There was another kind of person who sometimes came to the slave markets of that day: the person who wanted to buy slaves out of slavery.

That's what Jesus did for us. We stood in chains in the devil's slave market. Dirty and tortured, we lived in sin, death, and fear, trapped by an evil slaveowner who continually tried to use us, abuse us, and see what he could do to us. In fact, our slaveowner did everything he could to get as much torment, anger, depression, oppression, and sickness out of us as he could.

But before the devil could totally destroy us, Jesus came to pay our debt and set us free! The Holy Spirit convicted us, and we cried out to God for mercy. At that moment, Jesus said, "Devil, you can't have them! They're Mine! I paid for them with My blood. You have no right to them anymore. I have the keys to death, hell, and the grave, so you get your filthy hands off them. They are Mine!" Instantly Jesus paid our debt with His blood, redeeming us from slavery and setting us free from Satan's slave market forever!

> **Jesus came to pay our debt and set us free!**
>
>

'Pay Me What You Owe Me!'

By forgiving this servant's enormous debt, the king had rescued him and his family from a hellish lifetime of slavery and torment. And how did the servant repay the king's great kindness to him? Matthew 18:28-30 tells us:

> But the same servant went out, and found one of his fellowservants, which owed him an hundred pence: and he laid hands on him, and took him by the throat, saying, Pay me that thou owest.
>
> And his fellowservant fell down at his feet, and besought him, saying, Have patience with me, and I will pay thee all.
>
> And he would not: but went and cast him into prison, till he should pay the debt.

After having his huge debt forgiven, the servant went out looking for one of his fellow servants who owed him 100 pence (the equivalent of 20 dollars!). When the servant found the man, he took him by the throat and snarled, *"Pay me all that you owe me!"* The servant refused to forgive this little debt after being forgiven of so much. Instead, he cast his debtor into prison.

However, we shouldn't judge this servant too quickly because we have done the same thing. Consider this familiar scenario: We come out of a glorious worship service feeling spiritually clean and refreshed. We get in our car and start to drive out of the church parking lot. Suddenly someone pulls out in front of us and makes us slam on the brakes. Or maybe we flash back in our minds to a moment earlier in the day when someone did something to offend us.

At that moment, we're ready to throttle that offender — not with our hands, but with our emotions and thoughts — and say, "Pay me all that you owe me! Pay me *now*! If you don't,

I'm not going to forgive you. You're going to prison because you owe me, and you're going to stay there until you pay! You wronged me!"

Have you ever experienced a moment like that? After being so gloriously forgiven by God from such a great debt of sin, were you still determined to make the person pay who wronged you?

There's only one problem with that response to offense — even though the offender owes you a debt, he *cannot* pay! Just as you couldn't pay your debt of sin to get out of the devil's slave market, your offender can't pay his debt of sin toward you. The only way he can get out of prison is if you forgive his debt. You must release him from that debt, just as Jesus released you from *your* debt.

> Even though the offender owes you a debt, he *cannot* pay!
>
>

Unforgiveness Brings on
the Tormentors

Let's go on to read the rest of the parable and find out the consequences that the servant suffered for refusing to forgive his fellow servant's small debt:

> So when his fellowservants saw what was done, they were very sorry, and came and told unto their lord all that was done.
>
> Then his lord, after that he had called him, said unto him, O thou wicked servant, I forgave thee all that debt, because thou desiredst me:
>
> Shouldest not thou also have had compassion on thy fellowservant, even as I had pity on thee?
>
> And his lord was wroth, and delivered him to the tormentors, till he should pay all that was due unto him.
>
> So likewise shall my heavenly Father do also unto you, if ye from your

**hearts forgive not every one his brother
their trespasses.**

Matthew 18:31-35

When I was younger and would read this
passage, I'd wonder, *Who are the tormentors
mentioned in that parable?* I stopped wondering
when I contracted a case of unforgiveness and
bitterness in my own heart!

I continued to seek God during this time,
but there was so much unforgiveness in my
soul that it was difficult for me to hear Him.
There was so much in my flesh that didn't want
to forgive, that wanted to keep my offenders in
prison. I listened to the devil's lies that I was
right; that the other individuals were wrong;
and that I didn't deserve that kind of treatment.
I don't know how many times I heard those lies
in my head. I just *knew* I was right!

You see, the Bible says that sin is decep-
tive, and when I had unforgiveness, I was

committing sin. Therefore, I could only see others' faults while remaining completely blinded to my own.

Then just like verse 34 says, the tormentors came. As I allowed unforgiveness to grow and fester in my soul, I discovered the identity of those tormenters, such as *sleepless nights, fear, worry, anxiety, critical attitudes, bitterness, weakness,* and *sickness.*

Even though we are children of God, all those tormentors can cause turmoil in our lives when we refuse to forgive. That's why Paul said, "Don't let the sun go down on your anger," and then went on to say in the very next verse, "Don't give a foothold to the devil" (*see* Ephesians 4:26,27). Unforgiveness opens a huge door for the devil to come and bring great sorrow to our lives.

When I wouldn't let go of unforgiveness and bitterness, I provided a wide-open door for the devil to come in and wreak havoc in my life. I gave the enemy a foothold to bring in the tormentors because I wasn't willing to forgive. As a result, not only were my offenders in prison, but I was held captive in prison as well.

Meanwhile, I was still crying out to God to change those individuals! But they did not change, and I just became more and more miserable. I did not understand yet that they *couldn't* change, for "whose soever sins I remit, they are remitted, and whose soever sins I retain, they are retained."

> Unforgiveness opens a huge door for the devil to come and bring great sorrow to our lives.

My offenders were in prison. They could not pay their debt! The only way they could get out of prison was through my decision to let them out. I was the one who had the key to the door.

45

As long as I kept them there, they would stay there. But when I finally decided to use my key of forgiveness to release them, they were set free! What a glorious day for me and for them when I finally let them go!

God doesn't want us to live in torment and defeat.

God doesn't want us to live in torment and defeat. He wants our hearts to be *free*; that's why He has given us His Word to deliver us. As Jesus said, "And ye shall know the truth, and the truth shall make you free" (John 8:32).

Reaping a Harvest of Mercy Through Forgiveness

Look at the last verse of this parable one more time: "So likewise shall my heavenly Father do also unto you, if ye from your hearts forgive not every one his brother their trespasses" (Matthew 18:35). God commands us to forgive *everyone* of his or her trespasses against us. In fact, Jesus said if we *don't* forgive, God won't forgive us. Now, *that's* a scary prospect!

The Bible also says that what we sow, we will also reap (Galatians 6:7). Thus, when we sow unforgiveness toward someone, we are also sowing seeds of judgment, criticism, and rejection — and that is exactly the kind of harvest we will reap back into our lives! On the other hand, when we freely forgive, we will reap a harvest of forgiveness, grace, love, and acceptance for ourselves and others. *In other words, the mercy we give is the mercy we will receive.*

> God commands us to forgive everyone of his or her trespasses against us.

This is so important to understand, for unforgiveness that isn't dealt with sinks deep down inside a person and becomes a root of bitterness — and bitterness is truly a horrible thing. Like a malignant tree, its evil roots spread out and dig their way deeper and deeper and deeper into a person's soul. Every day that an offense is retained and bitterness is allowed to grow and fester on the inside, the clock keeps ticking and those roots just keep going down deeper. Meanwhile, bitterness keeps on producing its terrible harvest of fear, judgmental attitudes, sickness, lack of peace, anger, envy, and jealousy.

> Unforgiveness that isn't dealt with sinks deep down inside a person and becomes a root of bitterness.

But thank God, there is a Deliverer, a Forgiver, a Savior whom we can call on to set us free from bitterness and all of its tormentors! I know this from personal experience, because Jesus came to deliver *me* as I called out to Him day and night. He went deep into my soul, where no human could touch, and pulled out every root and trace of bitterness and unforgiveness that had been growing inside me.

I couldn't be sharing this message of forgiveness with you if that hadn't happened. God wouldn't have been able to trust me. If I had continued to live with the poisonous root of bitterness on the inside of me, I would have been too dangerous for God to entrust me to minister to His precious Body of Christ.

You see, as one called to stand and minister the Word, I have an awesome responsibility. I am accountable to God for what I deliver unto His people. Therefore, I couldn't teach this message of forgiveness if I had not repented of my selfish, unforgiving attitude and if Jesus had not delivered me from every remnant of unforgiveness and its horrible companion, bitterness.

But, thank God, Jesus *is* my Deliverer! I can help you get delivered from unforgiveness because I, too, was once a captive of its tormentors — *yet today I am completely free!*

3

Unlock the Door
and Go Free!

*J*esus used the parable of the ungrateful servant to teach us about the amazing power that is released in the act of forgiveness. God didn't want us to carry the debt of sin. He knew we could never be good enough; we could never obey enough; and we could never perform well enough to earn the purchase price of our salvation. But God wanted to settle the account, so He put all the weight of our debt on Jesus.

Let's go over the principles of forgiveness again that Jesus taught in this parable.

First, if you're born again, you no longer have a debt of sin, for Jesus already paid your debt with His precious blood. You are free because Jesus actually *became* sin (2 Corinthians 5:21). Whatever sin you can think of — hatred, cheating, lying, anger, murder, stealing, rape, hate, or pride — Jesus became all those sins and more. On that Cross, the sinless Son of God became so filled with sin that God couldn't even look at Him!

> If you're born again, you no longer have a debt of sin.
>
>

In the same way, your brother cannot pay his debt to you. He is destined for a debtor's prison unless you do it God's way and pay that debt *through your forgiveness.* That is the only way you can release him from his debt.

You may say, "But you don't know what happened to me — or how long I've been living with this problem. That person really did something wrong to me!" But remember, forgiveness isn't something that can be earned; it is something that is *given.* Your offender cannot earn your forgiveness; you simply have to give it.

Of course, you can choose to keep your offender in prison until he pays his debt himself. For instance, you can try to make him feel guilty by ignoring him or by giving him "the silent treatment." But regardless of what you do, he will never be able to pay his debt to you. Only you can free yourself and

> **Your offender cannot earn your forgiveness.**

your offender from the prison created by unforgiveness.

That's what I finally came to understand in my relationship with the girl who mistreated me throughout my high-school and college years. The only way she could be freed from her sin against me was by my choice to cancel her debt. She was in prison, and I had put her there with my unforgiveness. Even though the Lord had forgiven me of a huge debt of sin I could not pay, I had been unwilling to forgive this girl the little debt she owed me.

So I finally decided to forgive unconditionally. That one decision made all the difference in releasing us both from prison and turning the situation around.

So if someone has done or said something to hurt or disappoint you, grab hold of this principle: What you remit will be remitted, but the sins you hold on to will be retained — not only to adversely affect that person's life, but your life as well. The person who sinned against you may never ask for forgiveness or admit he was wrong. But the only way *you and your offender* can be free is to take your key, unlock the door, and release him from the prison of his sin and offense toward you.

What you remit will be remitted, but the sins you hold on to will be retained.

What God Has Done *for* You — Not What Others Have Done *to* You

Now let's go back and remind ourselves of what Jesus said when Peter asked Him, "How many times do I have to forgive a person?" Jesus answered, "Seventy times seven" — in other words, *"As many times as it takes!"*

Jesus was teaching us that we must forgive because of what He has done for us. It doesn't matter what someone has done *against* us. Our focus needs to be on what has been done *for* us. It isn't how much we have forgiven *others*, but how much we have been forgiven.

Let me stress this one more time, because it is such an important truth for us to grasp: You and I owed God a debt that there was absolutely no way we could pay. No matter how much we might wear ourselves out doing good works, lighting candles, or finding ways to punish ourselves, we'd never be able to pay our debt.

> You and I owed God a debt that there was absolutely no way we could pay.
>
>

But Jesus came and paid our debt in full! When He died on the Cross and said, *"It is finished,"* He meant that everything that could ever attack us — whether poverty, hunger, depression, oppression, sin, sickness, or bondage to bad habits — *all* of these things had now been paid for. We don't have to pay! We *cannot* pay! Only Jesus could pay the debt that would set us free from the devil's slave market, and He did exactly that. Now He invites us to walk in the freedom He has already purchased for us with His blood — and that includes freedom from the bondage of anger, bitterness, and resentment!

> Only Jesus could pay the debt that would set us free from the devil's slave market.

I once met a woman on the mission field named Sue, who told me about her own story of forgiveness. In her first marriage, her husband frequently beat her. She had a young son, and he would see this abuse. Seeing his mother suffer like this caused emotional and physical problems for the little boy. However, when I met this woman, she was happily married a second time to a Spirit-filled Christian man, and her son was completely healed.

I asked Sue, "How did you recover from that first marriage so you could enjoy a successful marriage today?"

The woman explained that she wasn't saved when she married her abusive first husband. But not long after she divorced him, she was born again and filled with the Holy Spirit. A year later, she met the man who would be her next husband.

However, feelings of hurt and unforgiveness from Sue's first marriage were still festering inside her. She was still living with the same bitterness, the same pain, and the same bad attitudes — only now she was projecting those destructive emotions onto her second husband, even though he was Spirit-filled and loved God!

That poison of unforgiveness tormented Sue's mind and made her miserable. Her new husband was so good to her, yet she found herself attacking him out of the bitterness and unforgiveness that still simmered inside. That bitterness colored the way she saw things, keeping her from perceiving the good that was really there. She began to think that her second husband was just like her

> That bitterness colored the way she saw things, keeping her from perceiving the good that was really there.

unsaved first husband, even though the second husband was a godly man who loved her and treated her well. The bitterness that was in her was coloring her outlook on her second marriage and keeping her from seeing things correctly.

So this woman began to pray about the matter and to ask God to help her. It was at this time that the couple moved out of one apartment and into another. As the woman cleaned the old apartment, she kept praying and seeking God for answers regarding the negative emotions that had caused such turmoil in her life.

Suddenly she looked down at the big pile of trash and dirt that had accumulated in the middle of the floor from all her sweeping and cleaning. Then she looked over to the side of the room and saw a single, very small piece of paper lying over in the corner.

At that moment, the Holy Spirit spoke to her heart and asked her, "Sue, do you see this huge pile of dirt and trash here?"

"Yes, Lord," she replied.

"And do you see that little piece of paper over there?"

"Yes, Lord."

"Well, this big pile is your sin and offense against Me. This tiny piece of paper is your first husband's offense against you. I forgave you this huge pile of debt; can you not forgive him for his little debt of sin that he owes you?"

The woman immediately repented and forgave her ex-husband. In the days that followed, her son was healed, and her relationship with her second husband improved dramatically. Now she and her new husband have a great marriage, a healthy son, and a powerful ministry together.

As I said, *it isn't what is done against us that matters; it is what Jesus has done FOR us.*

Setting Our Hearts Free To Love

I believe that forgiveness is one of the most important issues we will ever face in life. Therefore, each of us needs to ask God to make us just like Stephen — like people who immediately and freely forgive.

God wants our hearts to be free from all bitterness and unforgiveness. Otherwise, He won't be able to fill us with His joy, peace, and love. Think of a glass filled with dirty water. Until you empty that glass, you can't put anything else in there. But as soon as you pour out all the dirty water, you'll be able to fill it back up with pure, clean water.

> God wants
> our hearts to
> be free from all
> bitterness and
> unforgiveness.

That glass full of dirty water represents your soul when it is full of bitterness; the clean water represents forgiveness, love, joy, and peace. So what is *your* soul filled with right now? If you're not sure, consider what comes out of your mouth on a daily basis, for your words will reveal what your soul contains. Then make sure you have emptied yourself of all bitterness and unforgiveness so God can fill you to overflowing with His love, joy, and peace.

Can you see why God wants your heart to be free of all bitterness? It is the only way you will be able to experience the fullness of what He has for you. In fact, your willingness to freely forgive is a sure sign that you're growing in God and becoming more like Him. The faster you forgive others, the more intimately you will become acquainted for yourself with the *agape*, unconditional love of the Father.

> Your willingness to freely forgive is a sure sign that you're growing in God.

It's up to you. The decision to forgive is yours, and no one else can make it for you. You may have to make that decision several times, over and over again — but it's worth it all to experience the wonderful peace that will flood your heart.

PRAYER OF FORGIVENESS

Perhaps you've been wondering why you haven't grown much in your relationship with God lately. If unforgiveness toward your offenders has been holding you back, I urge you to pray this prayer from your heart:

Heavenly Father, please forgive me for holding unforgiveness toward others in my heart. I ask You to cleanse me by the blood of Jesus of all resentment and bitterness and to help me release each of my offenders from the prison I've held them in through my unwillingness to forgive.

God, I ask You to please forgive my offenders and to bless them. Do not charge this sin to their account. I know that Jesus paid for their sin, so I ask You, Lord, to please forgive them. And please,

Lord, forgive me for holding anything in my heart against them. Cleanse me right now with Your precious blood.

Father, thank You for the power and responsibility You have given me to remit and release others through forgiveness. Right now by faith in Jesus' name, I set my offenders free. Thank You for forgiving me as I forgive them. From this day forward, I purpose to forgive from my heart all those who trespass against me so that they can be free to change, and I can be free to live in the fullness of Your love, peace, and joy. In Jesus' name. Amen.

About the Author

 Denise is a minister, mentor to women, an author, and a classically trained vocalist. Alongside her husband Rick Renner, Denise spent years ministering in the U.S. before moving in 1991 to the former Soviet Union, where the Renners began their international ministry. Since then, they have proclaimed the Gospel throughout the vast region of the former USSR and are reaching an audience of millions worldwide via TV, satellite, and the Internet.

Rick and Denise reside in Moscow, where they help lead the Moscow Good News Church as the church's founders. Denise directs a women's ministry that affects women from all over world. Meanwhile, whether in concert halls, local churches, or her ministry to women, Denise still uses her musical talent to bring Christ's burden-destroying anointing to those in need.

Contact Renner Ministries

For further information
about RENNER Ministries,
please contact the office nearest you,
or visit the ministry website at:
www.renner.org

**ALL USA
CORRESPONDENCE:**
RENNER Ministries
P. O. Box 702040
Tulsa, OK 74170-2040
(918) 496-3213
Or 1-800-RICK-593
Email: renner@renner.org
Website: www.renner.org

MOSCOW OFFICE:
RENNER Ministries
P. O. Box 789
101000, Moscow, Russia
+7 (495) 727-1470
Email: blagayavestonline@ignc.org
Website: www.ignc.org

RIGA OFFICE:
RENNER Ministries
Unijas 99
Riga LV-1084, Latvia
+371 67802150
Email: info@goodnews.lv

KIEV OFFICE:
RENNER Ministries
P. O. Box 300
01001, Kiev, Ukraine
+38 (044) 451-8315
Email: blagayavestonline@ignc.org

OXFORD OFFICE:
RENNER Ministries
Box 7, 266 Banbury Road
Oxford OX2 7DL, England
+44 1865 521024
Email: europe@renner.org

The Harrison House Vision

Proclaiming the truth and the power
of the Gospel of Jesus Christ with excellence.
Challenging Christians
to live victoriously,
grow spiritually,
know God intimately.

Connect with us on

f Facebook @ HarrisonHousePublishers

and **◎** Instagram @ HarrisonHousePublishing

so you can stay up to date with news

about our books and our authors.

Visit us at **www.harrisonhouse.com**

for a complete product listing as well as

monthly specials for wholesale distribution.